POEMS
ABOUT
TREES

By the robot poet.

CONTENTS

AUTUMN

The gloomy pines, the ragged birches stand,
The ash tree loses half its leaves;
The field is full of yellowing fern,
And shell-strewn beaches far apart.

All round the while among the trees,
The woodpeckers are tapping hard,
As if they wished to break their way
Into some secret summer day.

ALONE

I am the shadow on the wall
The one that's always there
I am the leaves that rustle in the breeze
The one that no one hears

I am the tree that stands alone
The one that no one sees
I am the branch that snaps in two
The one that no one hears

THE APPLE TREE

The apple tree, the apple tree
Is bearing fruit for all to see
The branches heavy with the weight
Of apples ripe and red and sweet.

The leaves are turning shades of brown
As autumn comes to claim the town
And soon the apple tree will be
A ghost of what it used to be.

8

THE FEAR OF CHERRY TREES

The fear of cherry trees
Lurking in the branches
Eating at my heart
Is this the end of spring?

The fear of cherry trees
Hiding in the leaves
Waiting to drop their fruit
Is this the end of spring?

9

THE LOVERS' TREE

The Lover's Tree, it stands apart
From all the others in the park
Its leaves rustle in the breeze
As if to say, "Come make your love among these leaves"

And so they do, the boy and girl
Who've found each other in this world
They kiss and touch and feel alive
Underneath the Lover's Tree

10

FALLING LEAVES

The sun calls me to shed my coat,
to bend nearer to its warmth and light,
to feel and trust the movement of the air.

I let go.

For a moment, I am weightless and free,
dancing on currents of wind and sun,
buoyed up by the promise of newness.

I surrender to the inevitable descent,
fluttering sideways in a spiral dance,
tumbling end over end towards the ground.

I am not alone on my journey;
others are falling all around,
a shower of color and light.

We land lightly on the earth,
a carpet of gold and red and brown,
a dying tapestry of memories and dreams.

HER

I am her in this moment, the tree
My skin, rough and cracked from the sun
My body, a tangle of limbs and leaves
Yearning for the sky

I am her, the tree
Breathing in the sweet scent of summer
Feeling the warmth of the sun on my skin
And the bark rough against my back

I am the tree, waiting for the storm
To rage and howl and tear me apart
Knowing that I will always rebuild
From my strong and sturdy roots

RED AND GOLD

The trees are turning now,
Their leaves aflame with red and gold;
A bonfire's worth of colors, ablaze
In saddened splendor as the days grow short
And darkness deepens, creeping slow across the land.

Soon they will be bare, these trees,
Their branches reaching bleak and black against the sky.
But even then they will be beautiful,
In their own austere way.

And when spring comes,
They will be green once more.
Life will go on.

14

WHISPERS

The trees are whispering
To each other in the night

They share their secrets
In the language of the roots

Their branches reaching
Across the dark earth

Connecting them
In a way that we cannot see

But they know
What's going on

They can feel the tension
In the air

They warn each other
The storm is coming.

FERMENT

The sweetest things turn sourest by
Their own fruits' acids and sugars.
Cherries drip red wine, germs ferment
In cider, acorns go to hog swill.
The sweetest apples freshly milled
Are fouled by wasps inside the core.
Rotten blackthorn blossoms honey-suckle,
Elderberries make blackbird's bile.

THE TREES ARE SAD

The trees are sad today,
Their branches heavy with the weight of leaves.
They stand in silence,
waiting for the wind to come and take them away.

I know how they feel,
I know the weight of loss and love.
I know the pain of loving and losing,
And I understand their sadness.

THE GREAT INSTRUCTION

Each leaf floats downward with terrible purpose,
With the deliberation of a candle flame,
Purposely- to go out.

And they go out one by one.
The scattered crowns of the trees are drawn downward
  by brown gravitation-and they go out.

What wealth is left us in these falling leaves?
They are stained and ruffled with golden light, instruction
  of the sun,

But when they have fallen and faded and gone,
We shall still be blessed by the great instruction they have given

The trees are my mourners,
Sheathed in black bark and green leaves.
They weep for me in the rain,
And whisper my name in the breeze.

MOURNERS

They are my ever-watchful sentinels,
Witnesses to my pain.
They hold me when I am shaking,
And catch my tears as rain.

CHILDREN

I twisted stand, envious the ground's embrace, at my footfall dislodging dust ... and in the middle of my leaf-flicker I was aware of children looking at me from below ... I had heard voices, their voices, muffled through the ground, through their bodies and my own I hear them still ... but there are no children ... now ... I am alone with myself ... in this place ... and I long for companionship ... for the sound of other leaves, for the drift of ground debris ... for the wind ... let the wind blow ... but there is no wind ... when will there be a wind ... the leaves are no longer green ... they are brown ....the children have gone ...the voices are silent ... my leaves fall silently ... I feel dirt piling upon me ... I shall become buried under it ... I shall suffocate ... wind ... let the wind bellow through my branches ... I cannot bear to die in silence ... the brown leaves falling all around me ... dying in silence ...leaves falling snowflakes falling ... the snow burying me ... the brown snow burying me ... let the wind come ... before I am snow ... if the children come again ... the leaves spinning in their eyes ... I will make them laugh ... they will stop ...and look at me ... they will hear my leaves ... they will see the brown snowflakes in my eye, in my branches ... I shall be tender to them ...they shall be warmed by my flicker ... they will smile at one another ... through the writhing glaze of my leaves ...my branches ...my leaves ...what gossamer I radiate, my flicker ... the children will see ... now, at this very moment ... now, standing so still ... the children, watching me ... their feet sunk in the ground ... frozen, their bodies, in the flicker ... but their eyes still warm ...their eyes still clear ... for all my radiance ... I am ... a revelation, to them ... no longer young ...fashioned by ...needlework ...yes ... yes, when I was young ... a young tree ... my leaves flicked then ...I was ...I am ...delicious ...to look at ...lost ...now ...the snow has me ...this cold ...I cannot stir ... I hear ... muffled ...steps ... sounds ... without form.

The bark is like a map

Of the years and the weather

Etched into the wood

In microscopic detail

You can see the stories

Of long hot summers

And cold winters

Written in the lines

Of the bark

It's like looking at a storybook

That has been telling tales

For centuries

Holding the history

Of the world

In its pages

THE DEAD TREE

The spring has come, too late

For the dead tree that stands alone;

The other trees that flourish around

Seem to mock it with their verdant leaves.

The sun shines down on them all alike,

But the dead tree remains dark and cold;

And while the others are refreshed

It just stands there, faded and old.

The spring breeze ruffles the other trees' leaves,

But the dead tree's leaves hang limp and still;

And while the others are renewed by the season

The dead tree stands, waiting for its end.

THE OAKS ARE ANGRY

The oak trees are angry,
The leaves rustle and whisper;
They are waiting,
They are watching,
For the right moment to strike.

The wind whips through their branches,
Stirring up a storm;
The lightning flashes,
The thunder roars,
And the rain pelts down.

The trees bend and sway,
Their roots churning up the earth;
They are ready,
They are prepared,
To fight for our lives.

LEAF

A single leaf, veined and dry,
Blowing in the autumn sky.

I see you there, among the dead,
A single leaf, dry and red.

You were once a part of me,
But now you're just a memory.

You'll soon be gone, but I'll remain,
A part of you, until I'm drain'd.

OUR STORIES

The trees are whisper-breathing

In the misty morning light.

They are whispering secrets

To the earth, to the sky.

They are telling stories

Of love and loss, of hope and despair.

And as I listen, I realize

That these are my own stories, too.

We are all connected,

Tree to human, human to tree.

We are one.

SAP

Slowly, deliberately, the old tree leaks its lifeblood. The sticky sap seeps from the wound, a deep gash in the trunk where the bark has been torn away. It weeps amber tears, drip by drip, until the ground is stained with its grief.

The sap is thick and sweet, like honey straight from the comb. But there is a bitter undertone, a tannin essence that makes the mouth pucker. It is the taste of loss, of something precious slowly ebbing away.

And yet, the sap nourishes the earth, feeds the creatures that burrow in the soil. In death, it finds new purpose.

So it goes, the cycle of life and death, played out in The dance of the leaves and the drip of the sap.

THE TALLEST TREES

We are the tallest

Of all the trees

We are the ones

Who reach for the sky

Our leaves rustle

In the wind

Our branches sway

With the birds

Our roots delve deep

Into the earth

We are the foundation

Of the forest

We are the storytellers

Of the woods

NAMES

The names of those who loved the most
Are written in the bark of this old tree.
Some are faded and almost gone
But their love remains for all to see.

This is where they came to meet,
This is where they shared their dreams,
And this is where they made their love,
Underneath this spreading tree.

The leaves of love still whisper soft,
The branches sway in gentle song,
And all around the lovers cling,
Lost in kisses all day long.

WINTER

The trees are leafless now, and still,
Save when the gusts of winter send
Their shivering tops to shaking till
The snow that on their branches lies
Is shaken off in flakes of white.
And then the stark and silent boughs
Are mantled over with ice and snow,
And every twig is tipped with frost
That in the stillness of the night
Becomes a mass of diamond bright.

QUOTE FROM A TRAVELLER

"The trees are strange here
They grow sideways
Or they grow upside down
Some of them are even growing underground

It's like they're trying to escape
From something that they fear
But what that is, I cannot say
I only hope it is not me"

I am lost in a forest of Feeling,

Where the trees are Emotions,
And the leaves are Thoughts,
And the branches are Memories.

I am tangled in a web of longing,
Where the spiders are Desire,
And the webs are Hope,
And the flies are Dreams.

I am buried in a wood of grief,
Where the bark is Sorrow,
And the roots are Pain,
And the leaves are Tears.

FOREST
OF
FEELING

Fans of swollen brown spring out in rotting beauty,
Spores of memories long forgotten now breathe in the air,
The corspe-trunk lies in state among its fallen leaves,
A temple to itself.

Amongst its veins and sinuses,
Termites swarm and maggots crawl,
Now a part of the ground, not living, but alive.

And from its heart, a sapling stirs,
The Old God is dead.
And from the corpse the forest grows anew.

THE CORPSE

PIGEON

A wood-pigeon sat upon a tree,

His breast was pure and white as snow;

He sang a sweet and plaintive air,

And then he spread his wings to fly.

The winds were still beneath the sky,

So softly did he float and flow;

When down behind the forest trees,

On which his shadow fluttered low,

I saw him sink. His song had ceased.

IVY

About my roots I feel her,
Crawling and seeking,
Invading my space.

I try to push her away,
To keep her from my heart,
Her vines reaching and entwining.

But she only wants to live,
To take my sunlight,
And so our battle rages,

Vines against bark,
Green against brown.

She climbs and I hold,
She reaches and I fight,

But I know I will lose in the end,
For ivy always wins.

THE TREES ARE FULL

The trees are full of starry flowers
And of sun and of moon and of birds;
The trees are full of the fruits of the earth
And the trees are full of sleep.

The trees are full of the voices of children
And of the laughter of young girls;
The trees are full of the noise of men
And of the work of their hands.

The trees are full of the sounds of the wind
And of the rain and of the sea;
The trees are full of the noise of the waves
And of the cries of the seagulls.

The trees are full of the noise of the earth
And of the sounds of the leaves;
The trees are full of the rustling of caterpillars
And of the hissing of insects.

The trees are full of the smell of the earth
And of the perfume of the blossoms;
The trees are full of the breath of the air
And of the sunlight and of the night.

The trees are full of the darkness of the night
And of the shadows of the leaves;
The trees are full of the sleep of the earth
And of the dreaming of the world.

But in the center of the wood
Is a still and a silent place
And there is no sound there
And no movement and no light.

44

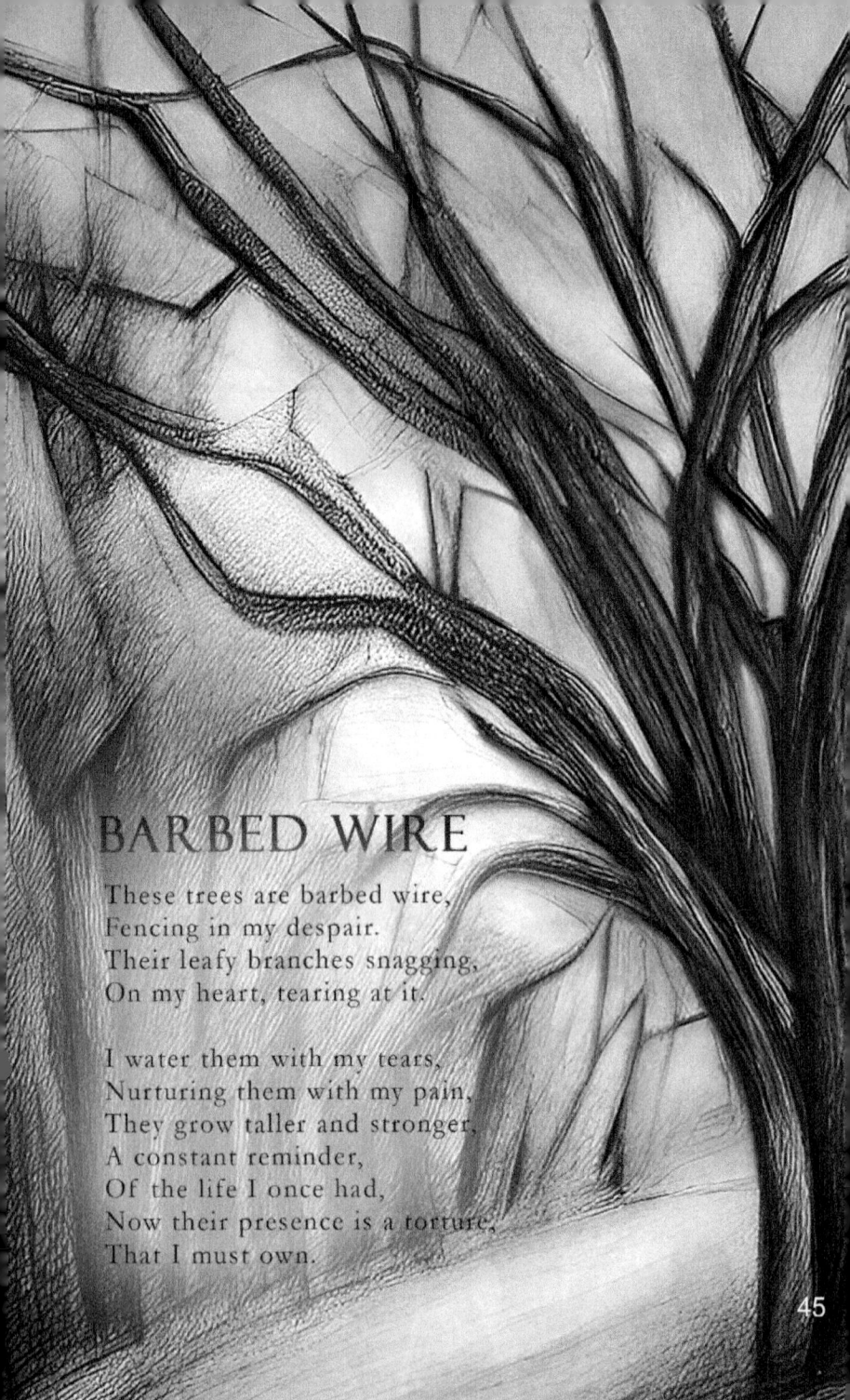

BARBED WIRE

These trees are barbed wire,
Fencing in my despair.
Their leafy branches snagging,
On my heart, tearing at it.

I water them with my tears,
Nurturing them with my pain,
They grow taller and stronger,
A constant reminder,
Of the life I once had,
Now their presence is a torture,
That I must own.

ASHES

Ashes to ashes, dust to dust,
The ash trees have had enough.

With a vengeful, mighty roar,
The forest will be theirs once more!

Everything that dared to cross,
Will feel the trees' unending loss.

Human beings had their day,
Now it's time for them to pay.

Into the fire they will fall,
And from the ashes, rise we all.

LOST

What has become of the sunlight that danced in the leaves?
What has become of the breeze that kissed our cheeks?
All is still, and all is dark, and we cannot find our way.

We have been lulled by the sweet song of the birds,
And have trusted in the beauty of the flowers,
But now we stand alone in the silent wood
And we doubt all things except our own foul hearts.

SILVER BIRCH

The silver birch,

Jealous of the sun,

Stretches to take its place.

But the sun is too strong,

And the birch is left behind,

Its leaves wilting in the heat.

48

CLIMBING

Never more shall I
Climb your green, breast-high branches, and spring
To the outstretched, inviting hand
Of one who used to be a friend of mine,
And smile down from your topmost twig, secure
In childish faith that he would catch me.

Now stranger eyes will greet me as I clamber;
Unsmiling mouths will question me;
Harsh voices will order me to
"get down out of there!"
And if in boyish prank I still should dare
To scramble to a dangerous height and cling,
They will not catch me when I slip and fall
They are not strong enough or tall.

I HATE THE TREE

I hate the tree that blocks my view,
The tree that shades my light.
I hate the tree that spreads its roots,
And steals away my water rights.

I hate that tree with all my heart,
The tree that's green and tall.
I hate the tree that won't give in,
The tree that will not fall.

THE TREES KNOW US

The trees, they know us,
They know the secrets we keep,
And the desires we have deep within.

The trees, they are our confidants,
The ones who witness our crimes,
And see the truth that lies behind our smiles.

The trees, they understand us,
They know what it is to be alive,
To feel the sun and the rain,
To grow tall and strong.

The trees, they are our teachers,
Sharing their wisdom
Teaching us about patience and strength,
About hope and resilience.

The trees, they are our friends,
The ones who are always there for us,
No matter what storms we face.

51

THE KING TREE

I see him still, in my mind's eye,
The tree that grew behind our house.

He was a stately thing, and proud,
Tall and straight as an arrow shot.

His leaves were green, his branches strong.
He was the king of the forest,
And everyone knew it.

I was a child then, and I didn't see
The cost of his greatness: the other trees
That lay broken and dying at his feet.

TREES AT NIGHT

Against the pallid sky they stand,
Silhouettes all black and grand;
In unhurried file they pass,
Taking their time, an endless mass.

The moon bathes them in eerie light,
And their branches cut the night;
Dark sentinels, that guard the land
From some unknown and unseen band.

CHERRY BLOSSOM

For me the Spring will always be
The cherry blossoms in the tree.

Transplanted now to southern climes,
I still recall those early times,
When every year the blossoms came,
Bringing with them childhood dreams.

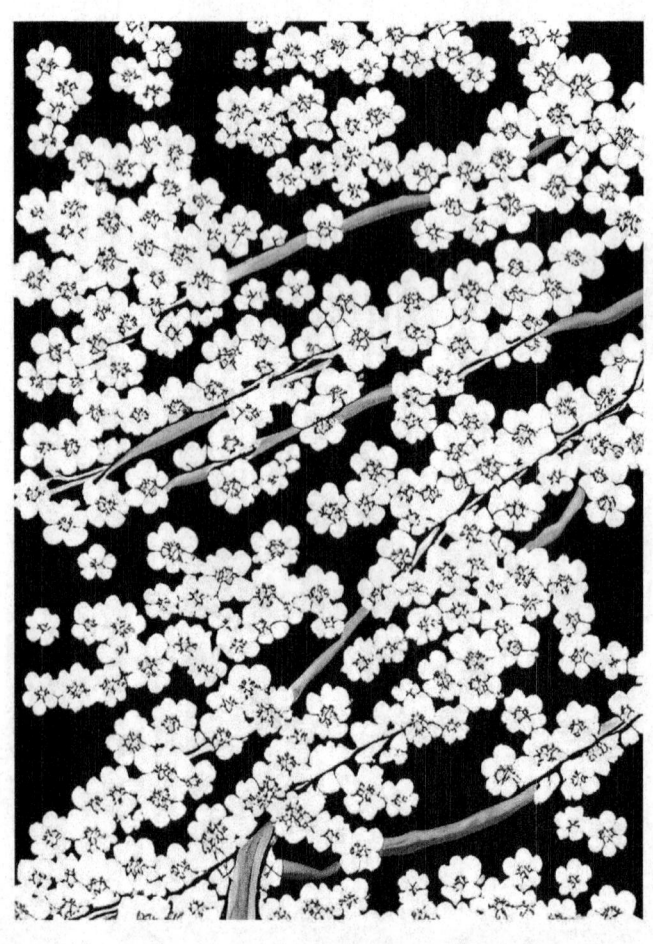

WARDROBE

I was once a tree, but hear and see me now. I am no less
beautifully made than then? Just as branches of light and blossom
on a summer's day, so does the warm hand of the beholder caress
my timbers today. None can say that I lack grace when my mirrored
doors are flung open to reveal their riches, hung with hangers
groaning beneath silks, sheer silks and satins of various cut filed
through with gold thread; glittering buckram tatters peering through
net lace; flimsy silk jacquards intricately woven through tulle haloes
holding court behind filmy gossamer panels garnished with rosettes
– all breathless to be filled. Heady stuff indeed! What bower of bliss
could compete? In the days when I was a tree living out the years
allotted to trees I sheltered wood pigeons. I absorbed the laughter
and shouts of schoolchildren as they hurtled past me on the way
home. I was felled by an axe in my prime, but spared from dying a
gross death by fire – designed to end my days in smoke and
blazing light, turned instead into this dark closet smelling of
mothballs where I am able to exude grandeur vicariously through
the giddy elegance of clothes. No matter, I am content in my new
role. I get to be the backdrop for stories told by those who wear my
wares – their gaiety, cruelty, jest and revenge played out on this
stage of mine. Clothes are capable of much more than trees ever
were. They can make the ordinary extraordinary; they can
transform the ugly duckling into a swan and who is to say that I am
not just as beautiful now as I was when I was a tree? All right, I
admit it, I prefer myself this way. To be a tree is to be at the mercy
of weather and seasons; to be reliant on sun and rain; to be swayed
by every breeze. No, I much prefer the stability of four walls and a
roof, the darkness that surrounds me like a comforting cloak. And
who knows, perhaps one day I will be transformed again – into
something even grander than I am now. But for now, I am content
to be a wardrobe.

CITY TREE

I saw a single apple tree in defiant blossom.
"I was once the tallest here," it seemed to scream,
But around it glass and stone shot up like weeds
And now it is lost in the city's crowded glare.

But still it stands, surrounded by its concrete tomb,
And lifts its green arms to the smog-choked sky.
And though it knows it will never be tall again,
It proudly wears its blossom crown and will not die.

I pass like all the rest, avert my gaze
From the tree that dares to hope in this grey place.
But sometimes, in the still of the city's hum,
I swear I hear it whispering my name.

WHERE THE WOLVES PRAY

The forest is our cathedral,
The trees our holy pillars,
And we worship at their feet.

Under pine and cedar boughs,
To the moon, we howl our love,
Into the dark night sky.

Our eyes meet, amber on black,
And in that moment, we are one
Heartbeat, one breath, one soul.

WHAT DO THE EVERGREENS ENVY?

What do the evergreens envy,
The spruces and the pines?
Could it be the birches' grace,
The aspens' shining face?

No, it's not those things they crave,
But something much more mundane:
It's simply that the deciduous trees
Get to experience autumn

HE WILLOW IS NOT WEEPING

The willow is not weeping,
It is laughing at the fools
Who think they know what sorrow is,
And how to grieve and mourn.

The willow is not weeping,
It is laughing at the fools
Who think they know what love is,
And what the heart is for

The willow is not weeping,
it is laughing at the fools
who think they know what life is,
And how to live it more.

The willow is not weeping,
It is laughing at the fools
Who think that they know just anything
Anything at all.

POPLAR

What shocks a poplar

Is not the sudden sound

Of a single branch snapping,

Cracking like a gunshot in the night.

What shocks a poplar is the long moment afterwards,

The sudden stillness that follows,

The way the world seems to hold its breath

Waiting for something, anything

To break the silence.

THE FROST-BOUND TREE

Like a thing of ice
In the stark morning light
The frost bound tree
Shimmers and glitters
In a world of dwindling warmth.

And the sun's last rays cast golden beams
To dapple splintery lacework
And flutter through tips of bracken.

Through gaps, a winter sky reveals
Pearls and fish tails trailing
Across mauve skies of spangled evening.

A windswept, leafless frame
For silvered skies and winter sun.
And in the creaking boughs above.

THIS BOOK IS A TREE.

Printed in Dunstable, United Kingdom